HOW DO RACE CARS WORK?

CAR BOOK FOR KIDS
CHILDREN'S TRANSPORTATION BOOKS

Speedy Publishing LLC
40 E. Main St. #1156
Newark, DE 19711
www.speedypublishing.com
Copyright 2017

All Rights reserved. No part of this book may be reproduced or used in any way or form or by any means whether electronic or mechanical, this means that you cannot record or photocopy any material ideas or tips that are provided in this book.

In this book, we're going to talk about how race cars work. So, let's get right to it!

There are many different types of race cars and auto races held worldwide. Formula One, also called F1, cars are the fastest of the different types of race cars and are designed for marathon courses. These cars are single-seat cars designed for the highest-class courses in the world. The "formula" stands for a set of specific rules that all participating cars and drivers must conform to. One of the races where drivers race these cars is the Grand Prix. The governing body that specifies all the rules for the F1 cars is the Fédération Internationale de l'Automobile or FIA for short.

In a lot of ways, these race cars aren't any different than the Ford car that might be parked in your garage. They have the same basic parts such as engines that run off internal combustion. They have transmissions and wheels as well as the all-important brakes. However, these cars aren't meant for everyday driving.

Even though they have the same basic parts as ordinary cars, they have been developed for only one thing and that is high speed. These cars can get to speeds upwards of 233 miles per hour, even though in a Grand Prix race the speeds might only be around 150 miles per hour.

CHASSIS

CHASSIS

The heart of the race car is its chassis. This is the main portion of the car to which everything is attached. Formula One cars feature a type of construction that's called "monocoque." The word comes from the French language and means that it's a singular shell, which simply means that the body is made out of one piece. Aluminum was formerly used but today some type of carbon fibers that are layered over a mesh made of aluminum or placed in resin are the usual construction materials. These materials produce a car that's very lightweight. It's also very strong and can withstand the tremendous forces acting on the car when it moves rapidly through the air.

The chassis has a special cockpit designed just for one driver. The cockpit must conform to the Formula One standards, which are rigorous. Each cockpit must have a minimum size and it must also be constructed with a floor that's completely flat. The seat is the only part that is customized for the driver and is created to fit him perfectly so he doesn't move when the car "flies" around the track.

ENGINE

Before the year 2006, F1 cars were run by huge three-liter size engines with 10 cylinders in two banks of 5 each. Then, the FIA, which is the governing body that specifies the rules, changed the specifications to a V8 engine, with a capacity of 2.4 liters. Even though this change meant that the power output of the engines decreased, these engines are still 900 horsepower.

As a comparison, the Jetta, a type of Volkswagen, has a 2.5-liter capacity, but only 150 horsepower. You might be able to drive a Jetta for over 100,000 miles before the engine would burn out, but an F1 engine really needs to be rebuilt after about 500 miles of racing. The reason is that the engine has to run at about 19,000 rpm or revolutions per minute. Running the engine at that rate puts a huge amount of tension and stress on its parts.

ENGINE

F1 cars don't use a typical gasoline either. F1 racing car teams use about 50 different types of gasoline blends and additives that boost power are not allowed. Any fuel that is used must meet the approval of the FIA standards.

In order for the engine's power to be transferred to the rear wheels a quality transmission is built into the car.

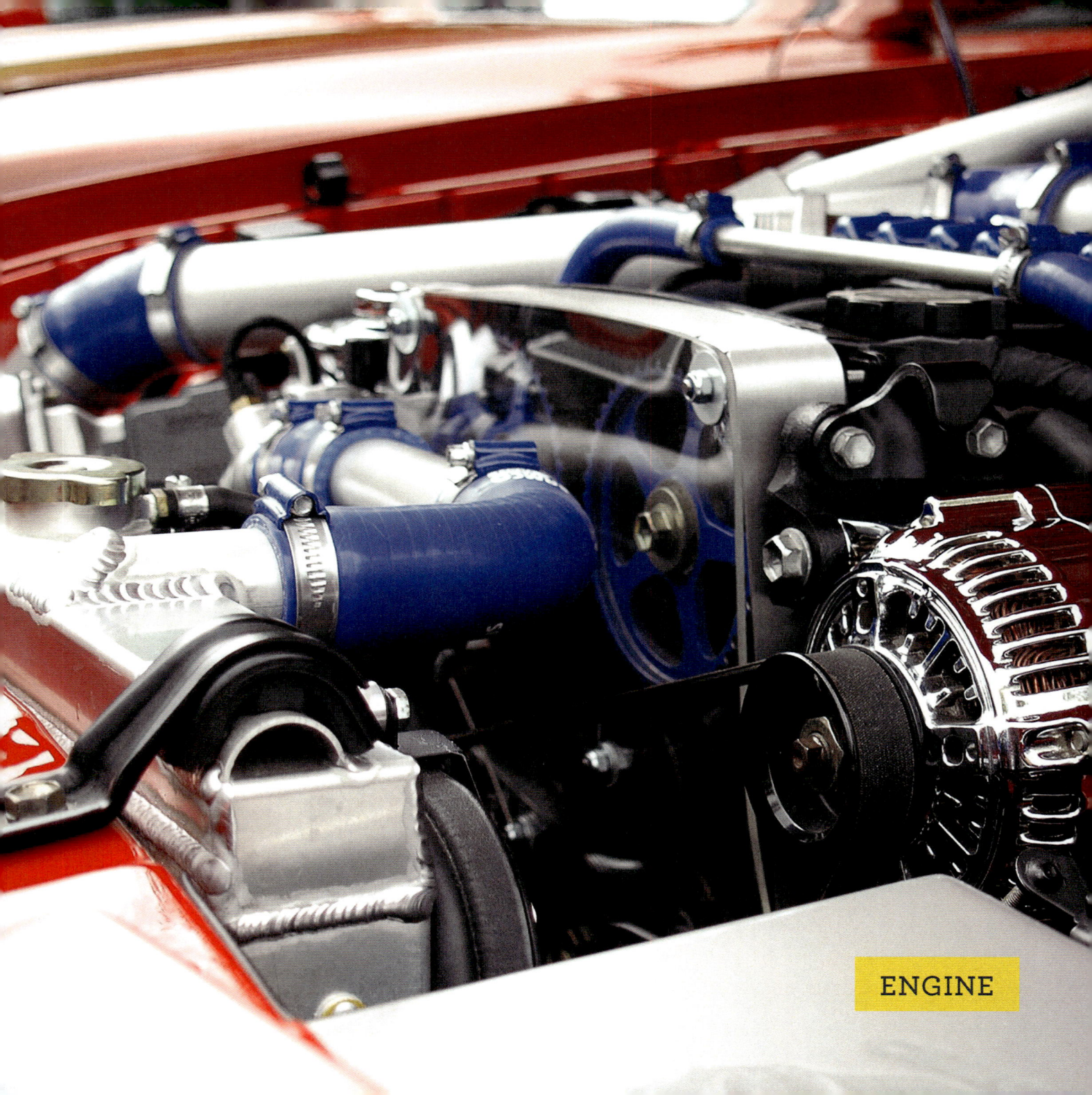

ENGINE

It is bolted to the back of the engine and includes these parts:

A GEARBOX

The gearbox can have a maximum of seven gears, but must have at least four forward gears. For a while, gearboxes with six speeds were popular, but now most F1s have seven. They also need to have a reverse gear. The gearbox is attached to a differential.

A DIFFERENTIAL

The differential gives the car the ability for the wheels to travel at varying speeds when the car is turning. The differential is attached to a driveshaft.

The job of the driveshaft is to send power to the car's wheels.

When the driver needs to shift gears in an F1 car, it's very different than shifting gears in an ordinary car with a manual transmission. Instead of the everyday "H-shaped" selector, there are paddles that are situated behind the steering wheel. If the driver wants to downshift, he uses the paddles on one side of the steering wheel, if he wants to upshift he uses the paddles on the other side. Although these cars can be built with automatic transmissions they have been deemed illegal by the FIA. One of the reasons is that the skill that a driver has shifting gears appropriately can be an advantage in winning the race.

AERODYNAMICS

An F1 race car has to have an incredibly powerful engine, but just as important is the overall design of the car. An aerodynamic design is critical to its success at attaining high speeds. To decrease the friction of the atmosphere as much as possible, F1 cars are designed to be low to the ground and quite wide. To increase the car's downforce, it needs four different parts:

Wings were first made part of the design in the 1960s. They have a similar function as an airplane's wings except they are supposed to produce the opposite effect. Instead of lifting the car off the track like an airplane, they are designed to push the car down onto the track. This is especially important for when the car is approaching a corner at very high speed.

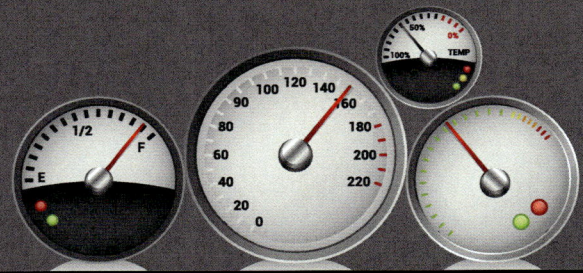

Most of the F1 cars have a design that is flat all the way from the nose cone to the line of the rear axle. Most designs have a diffuser. A diffuser is a device that has an upward curve under the engine and under the gearbox. It makes an effect that sucks air up and then sends it out toward the rear of the car.

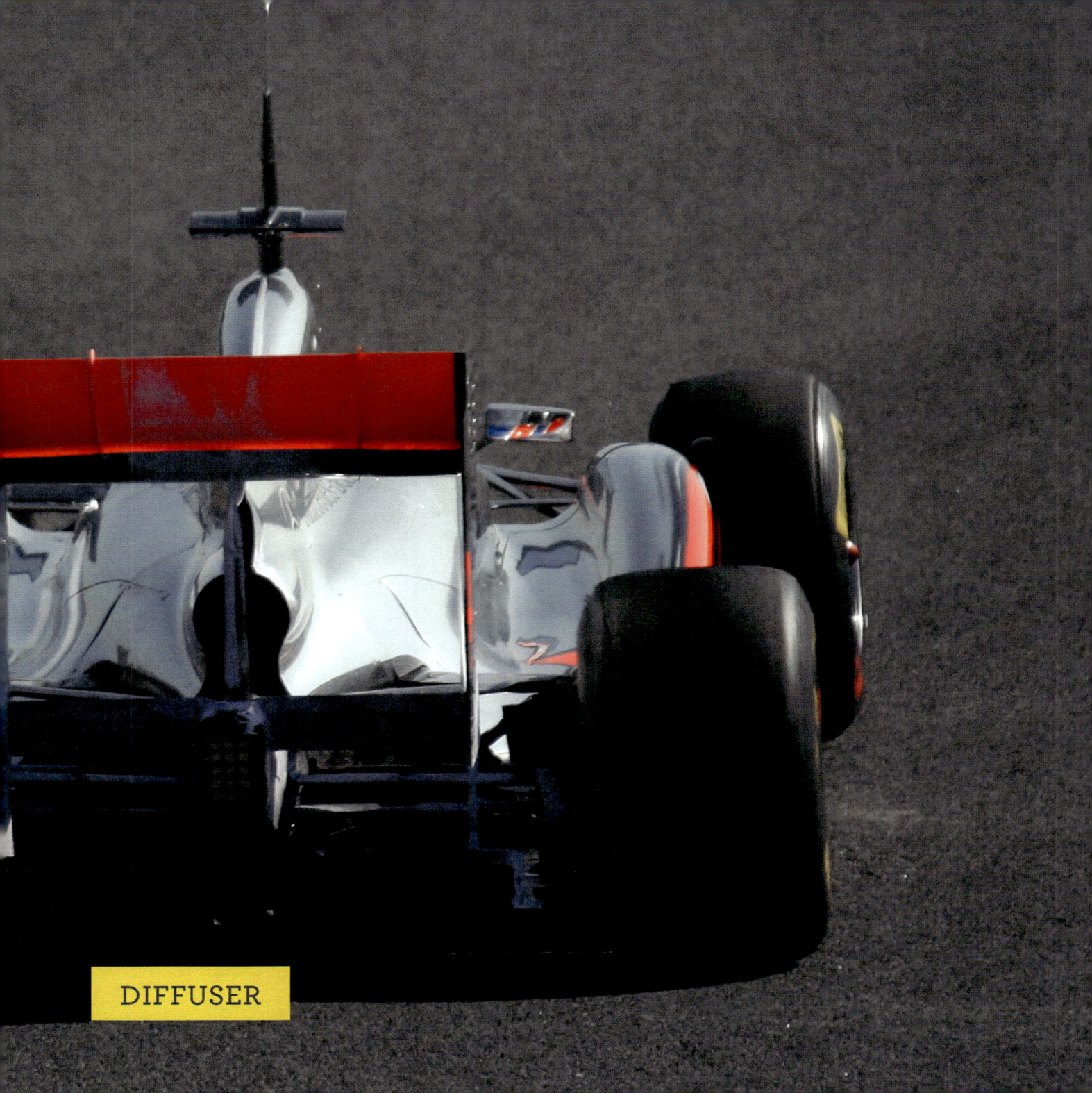
DIFFUSER

Endplates are small flanges on the front wings' edges that grab up the currents of air and direct them alongside the body of the car.

The barge boards grab up the air directed from the endplates and make it go faster in order to create more downforce.

With all these devices to create downforce, the end result is a force of over 5,500 pounds. The car only weighs about one-fourth of the downforce its design creates!

SUSPENSION

A suspension system on an F1 car has the same parts as an ordinary car. Most F1 cars have a type of suspension system called a double wishbone. Before the start of any race, the team responsible for the driver of a particular car will adjust and tweak the settings to make sure that the car is able to stop as well as take corners safely. It could mean life or death to the driver.

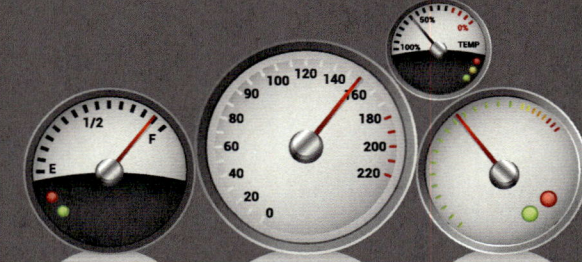

BRAKES

The brakes on an F1 race car are similar to those in ordinary cars except that they must be able to halt the car when it is traveling at very high speeds of 200 miles per hour or more. When the brakes are applied, they get very hot to the point where they actually glow red. Special discs made of carbon fibers and specially designed pads are used to reduce the wear on the brakes. They are effective up to temperatures over 1300 degrees Fahrenheit and are still very lightweight.

Holes positioned around the disc's edge make it possible for the heat to diffuse quickly. In addition, the cars have intakes for air that are on the outer part of each wheel's hub that are designed to cool the brakes down rapidly.

TIRES

In some ways, the tires are the most important part of an F1 car. They are the only part of the car that has contact with the road. Every part of the car can be working at maximum efficiency and effectiveness, but if the F1's tires don't travel well the driver and car can't win the race. Just like all the other parts of an F1 car, the approved standards are very specific.

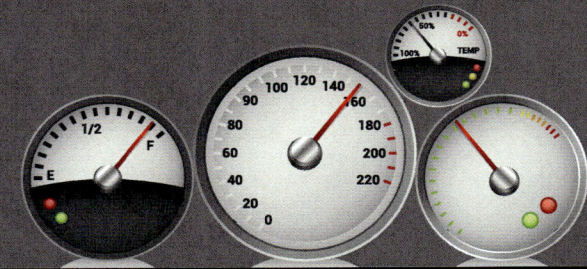

There are minimum and maximum widths for the tires as well as specifications for the tire grooves. The tires are composed of a type of rubber that is very soft so it will hold onto the road as much as possible. To perform at their best, the tires must be heated up before the race starts. These tires only last for 120 miles or so.

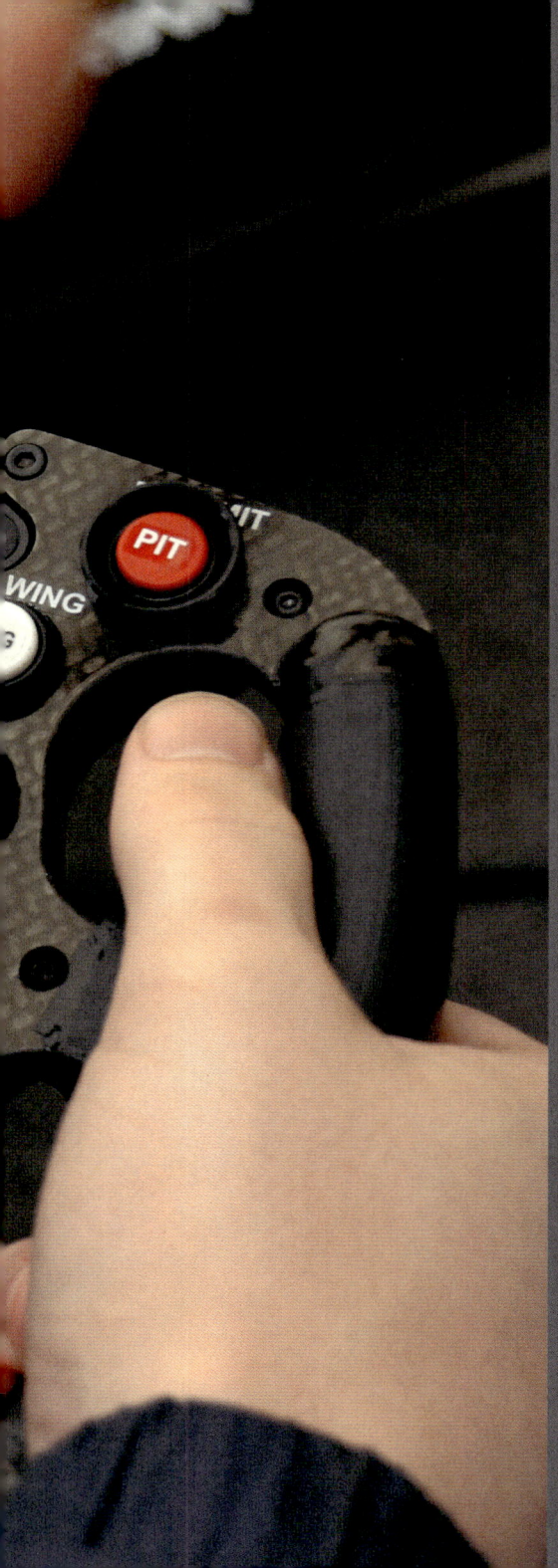

The wheel used for steering in an F1 car doesn't look like the one in an ordinary car at all. It looks more like a command hub with tons of buttons and switches. The driver can manage all aspects of the car with just a touch. The steering wheel is half of the width of the wheel in an everyday car.

The FIA rules specify that within five seconds a driver must make his escape from the car and only remove

the wheel used for steering. To make this possible, the wheel can be detached at its column for a quick getaway.

SUMMARY

Formula One race cars are designed for maximum speed and performance. They are built for marathon races and must conform to very specific standards as specified by the governing body called the FIA. They are the fastest cars in the world and can travel up to 233 miles per hour.

Awesome! Now that you've read about how race cars work, you may want to read about a famous driver who doesn't drive a Formula One car in the Baby Professor book Living the Fast Lane: The Jimmie Johnson Story.

Visit

www.BabyProfessorBooks.com

to download Free Baby Professor eBooks and view our catalog of new and exciting Children's Books

Made in the USA
Las Vegas, NV
20 November 2021